Bird Nests

by Heather Adamson

amicus readers 1

Amicus Readers are published by Amicus
P.O. Box 1329, Mankato, Minnesota 56002

Printed in the United States of America at Corporate Graphics,
North Mankato, Minnesota.

Library of Congress Cataloging-in-Publication Data
Adamson, Heather, 1974-
   Bird nests / by Heather Adamson.
      p. cm. – (Amicus readers. Our animal world)
   Summary: "Highlights different types of bird nests, showing where they are located
and what they are made of. Includes comprehension activity"–Provided by publisher.
   Includes index.
   ISBN 978-1-60753-009-1 (library binding)
   1. Birds–Nests–Juvenile literature. I. Title.
   QL675.A33 2011
   598.156′4–dc22

                                              2010007290

Series Editor   Rebecca Glaser
Series Designer   Kia Adams
Photo Researcher   Heather Dreisbach

Photo Credits
Alamy, cover; Corbis/Tranz, 6, 8, 10, 16, 20 (all), 21 (t), 22 (tl, tc, tr, bl); David
Cavagnaro/Getty, 4–5; Ludmila Yilmaz/iStockphoto, 12, 21 (m), 22 (bc); Michael
S. Quinton/Getty, 18–19; Photolibrary, 14, 21 (b), 22 (br); Roy Morsch/CORBIS, 1

1224
42010

10 9 8 7 6 5 4 3 2 1

Table of Contents

Birds build nests from things they find around them. Nests keep eggs and baby chicks safe.

An albatross builds its nest
with island grass and dirt.
Chicks can rest in the nest.

pebbles

Adelie penguins use pebbles to make their nests. The small pile of stones keeps the eggs and chicks off the mud.

Orioles weave strings and grass to make nests. Their nests hang from branches. Several chicks share one oriole nest.

Storks build their nests in high places. They use sticks and twigs to make their nests. Each year they add more sticks to their nests.

eave

Swallows build their nests with mud. Their nests tuck under ledges and eaves. Swallow chicks stay warm and dry in their nests.

Owls like to build their nests inside things. Holes in trees are great places for owl nests. They can sleep all day and hunt at night.

Birds build nests. Nests are good homes. What kind of nests have you seen where you live?

Picture Glossary

Adelie penguin
a penguin that lives in Antarctica and builds its nest out of pebbles

albatross
a sea bird that spends most of its time flying; Albatrosses only use their nests for breeding.

oriole
an orange songbird that weaves its nest from string and grass; Orioles usually build their nests in the fork of a tree branch.

owl
a bird that hunts at night; Owls have big eyes to help them see at night.

stork
a long-legged bird that likes to catch fish in shallow water

swallow
a small bird that eats flying insects

21

Match each bird to what it uses for its nest.

Adelie penguin

albatross

oriole

owl

stork

swallow

grass   mud

sticks   pebbles

hole in tree   grass and dirt

Ideas for Parents and Teachers

Our Animal World, an Amicus Readers Level 1 series, gives children fascinating facts about animals with lots of reading support. In each book, photo labels and a picture glossary reinforce new vocabulary. The activity page reinforces comprehension and critical thinking. Use the ideas listed below to help children get even more out of their reading experience.

Before Reading

- Ask children to think about why birds need nests.
- Look at the cover photo together. Ask children what they think is happening.
- Look at the picture glossary words. Tell children to watch for them as they read the book.

Read the Book

- Read the book to the children or have them read independently. Remind them to look at the photos for clues if they need help understanding the words.
- Show children how to use the features of the book such as the photo labels to help with reading.

After Reading

- Have children retell the kinds of things birds use to make nests. See if anyone can think of other things birds use to make nests.
- Ask children what kind of places birds build their nests. Have them tell of places that they have seen birds or nests.
- Talk about how a bird might build a nest. For example, look at the swallow nest on page 14. Ask them how they think the birds carry the mud.

Index

Web Sites

BIOKids—Kids' Inquiry of Diverse Species, Bird Nests
http://www.biokids.umich.edu/guides/tracks_and_sign/
build/birdnests/

Bird Nests
http://www.50birds.com/gnest1.htm

ZOOM—Activities, Science, Bird Nests—PBS Kids
http://pbskids.org/zoom/activities/sci/birdsnests.html